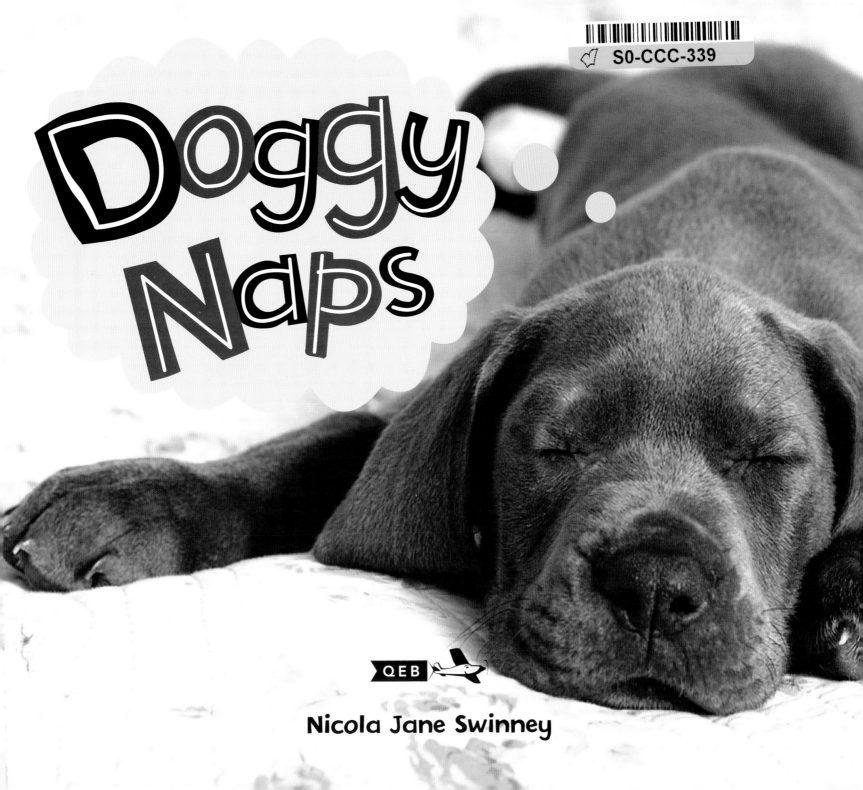

Doggy Naps

QEB

Nicola Jane Swinney

Quarto is the authority on a wide range of topics.

Quarto educates, entertains and enriches the lives of our readers—enthusiasts and lovers of hands-on living.

www.quartoknows.com

Editor: Emily Pither
Designer: Barbi Sido

First Published in 2017 by QEB Publishing, Inc.
an imprint of The Quarto Group.
6 Orchard Road
Suite 100
Lake Forest, CA 92630
T: +1 949 380 7510
F: +1 949 380 7575
www.QuartoKnows.com

A CIP record for this book is available from the Library of Congress.

ISBN: 978 1 68297 375 2

Manufactured in Shenzhen, China
RD102017

9 8 7 6 5 4 3 2 1

MIX
Paper from responsible sources
FSC
www.fsc.org   FSC® C101537

Contents

Afghan

🐾 Perfect puppy

Afghan puppies can be quite sneaky as they grow up, and are smart enough to steal objects from right under your nose! They are adorably awkward because their long legs grow unevenly—making them wobbly on their paws and likely to trip.

DOGGY NAPS

Afghans need lots of exercise to make their bones and muscles strong. After a long run, they will curl up like a cat and go to sleep.

🐾 Top dog

The Afghan is a very old breed that comes from Afghanistan, where it grew its long, silky coat to keep out the cold mountain air. The Afghan's coat comes in many colors and needs lots of brushing and grooming. Afghans are brave, gentle, and athletic.

FACT BOX
- Can weigh as much as 60 lb (27.3 kg)
- Lives for up to 12 years
- Needs at least 2 hours of exercise a day
- Loves a large house in the countryside

Did you know?

The first cloned dog was an Afghan.

5

Airedale Terrier

Z Z Z Z Z

Did you know?

Airedale Terriers were one of the first breeds to be used as police dogs in England.

🐾 Perfect puppy

Confident and clever, Airedale puppies like to play! They love children and will happily join in with games. Airedales keep their puppyish traits even when they've grown up, so they make fun pets to play with.

🐾 Top dog

As the largest of all the terrier breeds, the Airedale is known as the King of Terriers. They come from the Airedale Valley in Yorkshire, England, where they were bred to catch rats and otters. Airedales are very intelligent, and because of their short, wiry coats they are easy to keep clean.

FACT BOX

- 🐾 Can weigh as much as 65 lb (29.5 kg)
- 🐾 Lives for up to 13 years
- 🐾 Needs between 1 and 2 hours of exercise a day
- 🐾 Is happy in town or the country

DOGGY NAPS

The Airedale loves to sleep on its back, with its legs in the air!

Akita

Did you know?
There is an Akita museum in Japan!

🐾 Perfect puppy

Don't be fooled by the cute Akita—this cuddly puppy will grow into a big, strong dog that will guard you and your family. As a baby, it can be shy, and needs to meet lots of new people to gain confidence. It needs firm but kind handling from an early age.

🐾 Top dog

In Japan, the Akita was bred as a fighting dog. Because of its bravery, it was used to guard important people who trained it to hunt deer, wild boar, and even black bears. It is a strong and solid dog with a cute tail that curls over its back. The Akita doesn't bark very much, but will grunt, moan, and mumble at you!

DOGGY NAPS

Akitas can be very lazy and will sleep all the time if you let them!

American Cocker Spaniel

DOGGY NAPS

Cocker Spaniels are very intelligent and can be taught when it is their bedtime!

🐾 Perfect puppy

Loving and gentle, the American Cocker Spaniel is the ideal family puppy. It will be just as happy snuggling with you on the couch or playing with you in the back yard. American Cocker Spaniels have soft, wavy coats and love to wag their tails!

Did you know?

The word "spaniel" means "Spanish dog."

🐾 Top dog

There are several different types of Spaniel, including Field, Water, and Springer. The American Cocker Spaniel is very similar to the English Cocker Spaniel, but has a smaller body and a shorter muzzle. The American Cocker Spaniel is easy to train, loves long walks, and needs regular exercise.

FACT BOX

- 🐾 Weighs as much as 28 lb (12.7 kg)
- 🐾 Lives for up to 15 years
- 🐾 Needs more than 2 hours of exercise a day
- 🐾 Loves a small house but needs room to run around

11

Basset Hound

🐾 Perfect puppy

With their long ears and sad eyes, Basset puppies are adorable. But this breed needs lots of care because, like most hounds, they can be stubborn and slow to train. Basset Hounds make great family pets because they are calm and friendly.

DOGGY NAPS

Basset Hounds love lounging on the couch! They need lots of exercise to avoid gaining weight.

🐾 Top dog

The Basset Hound was first used as a hunting dog. Its short legs were probably an accident of breeding, but its size meant it could hunt through lots of undergrowth in heavy forests. The Basset Hound is a big dog on little legs!

Did you know?
The Basset was bred in France and that "bas" means "long and low" in French?

Beagle

🐾 Perfect puppy

A sweet little puppy, the Beagle's wide grin and soft brown eyes are hard to resist. Although they are pack dogs, Beagles make good pets because they are gentle and friendly. They are very cute and playful, but they can also be very naughty!

DOGGY NAPS

Beagles love to chase things and will do so in their dreams. Watch their legs "run" as they sleep!

🐾 Top dog

The Beagle is an old breed which used to be called the Glove Beagle or Pocket Beagle because the dogs were tiny enough to sit in your hand and small enough to fit in your pocket! Modern Beagles are much bigger, but they are still very cute. Beagles are very quick and love to exercise.

FACT BOX

- 🐾 Can weigh as much as 30 lb (13.6 kg)
- 🐾 Lives for up to 15 years
- 🐾 Needs up to 1 hour of exercise a day
- 🐾 Happy in a small house

Did you know?

During his time in the White House, President Lyndon Johnson kept two Beagles, named Him and Her.

Bernese Mountain Dog

Perfect puppy

This little puppy might look like a cute bundle of fluff, but it will grow into a big, strong dog! Bernese Mountain Dogs were once used to herd cows in Switzerland. They love to be with people and like working closely with their owners.

Did you know?
Some say that the white marking on its chest represents the cross on the Swiss flag.

DOGGY NAPS
The Bernese doesn't like to sleep in a kennel, it prefers to snuggle up with its owner.

🐾 Top dog

Bernese Mountain Dogs are very brave. In Switzerland, they were used to pull carts and search for people in avalanches—a very important job in the mountains. To keep warm, the Bernese Mountain Dog developed a lovely thick coat.

Bichon Frise

Did you know?
The Bichon Frise is thought to have lived on the island of Tenerife as far back as the 14th century.

Perfect puppy

This adorable little pup looks like a toy, and it will be happy to play with you all day! With its sweet, round face and curly white fluff, the Bichon Frise is one of the cutest breeds. It just loves to be with people and makes a wonderful family pet.

🐾 Top dog

The Bichon Frise was developed in France. "Bichon" means white dog in French and the word "frise" describes its coat's soft curls. With a curled double coat, Bichons don't shed, but require a lot of grooming, bathing, and trimming.

DOGGY NAPS
The Bichon Frise loves company and likes to cuddle before bed!

Border Collie

🐾 Perfect puppy

It may look like a black-and-white cuddly armful of mischief, but the Border Collie is a very intelligent dog. Border Collie puppies learn very quickly and are easy to train from a young age.

DOGGY NAPS

The Border Collie loves to snooze, but needs lots of exercise to wear it out first.

🐾 Top dog

The breed's name comes from the border between Scotland and England, and between England and Wales. It was bred to herd sheep and will still try to round up anything it sees—children, cats, and other dogs—nipping and nudging to get them into place!

Did you know?
The Border Collie is known for its intense stare, or "eye," which it uses to control its flock of sheep.

Borzoi

🐾 Perfect puppy

With long legs, wide eyes, and floppy ears, Borzoi puppies are adorable and always want to please. The Borzoi may be a little shy at first, but it is kind, gentle, and will be happy as a family pet.

Did you know?

The word "borzoi" means "swift" in Russian.

🐾 Top dog

The Borzoi is a tall, elegant dog and can be very fast. It comes from Russia and was bred to hunt wolves. Borzois were sent off in pairs which would hold the wolves down until the hunters on horseback caught up.

FACT BOX
- 🐾 Can weigh as much as 105 lb (47.7 kg)
- 🐾 Lives for up to 12 years
- 🐾 Needs at least 1 hour of exercise a day
- 🐾 Loves a big house with plenty of room to run around

DOGGY NAPS
The Borzoi grows into a tall dog and if you let it, will stretch out across the couch to relax!

Boxer

🐾 Perfect puppy

Boxer puppies love to play! The Boxer is one of the most loving breeds and it will always be happy to see you. It will waggle its cute little behind in delight, and give you a wide, adorable grin of greeting.

DOGGY NAPS

The Boxer doesn't know its own size! It is the world's biggest lap dog and will try its best to curl up on you for a nap.

🐾 Top dog

The Boxer was used to hunt bear, wild boar, and deer in the 19th century. Its early relatives were called Bullenbeisser, which meant "bull-biter." It is a big dog with a square head, and is very smart and strong. It also makes an excellent guard dog.

Did you know?

Unlike many other breeds, Boxers don't reach adulthood until they are three years old.

Chow Chow

Did you know?

Most dogs have pink tongues, but Chow Chows have blue-black tongues.

Perfect puppy

This little pup looks like a fluffy pompom, with a sweet face like a teddy bear. You could cuddle it all day, but it is fun to play with, too. The Chow Chow is one of the oldest dog breeds in the world, and comes all the way from Mongolia and China.

DOGGY NAPS

All puppies need their sleep, but even when full grown the Chow Chow will nap a lot.

🐾 Top dog

It may look cuddly, but the Chow Chow was bred to hunt. One Chinese emperor is said to have kept 5,000 Chow Chows for hunting. It is a big, strong dog and was used to guard precious items, too. In China it was known as "songshi quan," which means "puffy lion dog."

Corgi

🐾 Perfect puppy

With their short legs and long bodies, Corgi puppies are very cute. There are two types of Corgi: Cardigan and Pembroke. The Cardigan is the oldest variety and they have long tails which look like the sleeve of a cardigan.

Did you know?

The Queen of England loves Corgis and has kept them ever since receiving one as an 18th birthday present.

ZZZZZZ

DOGGY NAPS

Corgis are smart dogs and need to be kept alert, otherwise they will sleep all day!

FACT BOX

- Can weigh as much as 38 lb (17.3 kg)
- Lives for up to 15 years
- Needs at least 1 hour of exercise a day
- Happy in a small house and back yard

Top dog

There have been Corgi-type dogs in Wales for 3,000 years. An old Welsh fairytale says fairies ride short, long-backed dogs in a hunt across the night sky. Corgis may not be able to fly, but they are short and stocky. Despite their little legs, Corgis are speedy when they run.

Dachshund

🐾 Perfect puppy

The adorable Dachshund loves people, and it doesn't like being left alone. Include it in everything you do and it will be a happy little puppy. Dachshunds are very curious and adventurous, so they often get themselves into trouble, but it's hard to be angry with a dachshund because they're so cute!

Did you know?
In 1972, Waldi the Dachshund became the first mascot for the Olympic Games.

🐾 Top dog

The Dachshund comes from Germany, where it was used to dig into the ground to find badgers, rats, and rabbits. Its name means "badger hound" in German. It comes in three sizes: standard, miniature, and *kaninchen*—meaning rabbit in German—decided by the dog's chest measurement.

FACT BOX
- 🐾 Can weigh up to 30 lb (13.6 kg)
- 🐾 Lives for up to 15 years
- 🐾 Needs about 30 minutes of exercise a day
- 🐾 Happy in a little house or apartment

DOGGY NAPS
Dachshunds love to curl up for a nap in your bed under the sheets and blankets

31

Dalmatian

🐾 Perfect puppy

With striking spots and a wide, happy grin, the Dalmatian is an adorable and loving dog. Dalmatian puppies are quite small, but they grow up to be big, tall dogs. They have lots of energy and need plenty of exercise.

🐾 Top dog

Dalmatians were once used as carriage dogs to run alongside horse-drawn coaches, guarding passengers and keeping their luggage safe. Dalmatians are also very intelligent and need to be kept entertained, but their fun and goofy ways are hard to resist!

FACT BOX
- 🐾 Can weigh as much as 55 lb (25 kg)
- 🐾 Lives for up to 16 years
- 🐾 Needs at least 2 hours of exercise a day
- 🐾 Loves a large house and back yard to run around

DOGGY NAPS
For such a large dog, the Dalmatian can curl up very small when it's time for a nap.

French Bulldog

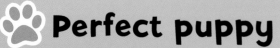 Perfect puppy

With its short, little legs and cute wrinkled face, the French Bulldog is a popular puppy! French Bulldogs have little bodies, but have big ears and round chocolate button eyes. French Bulldogs are great fun and love to play.

DOGGY NAPS
The French Bulldog doesn't like going to bed because it means being apart from its owners!

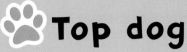 ## Top dog

In the 1800s there was a small breed known as the Toy Bulldog which was popular with the lace-makers of Nottinghamshire, England. When the Industrial Revolution threatened their jobs, the lace-makers went to France, taking their little dogs with them—which is why we now call them French Bulldogs.

FACT BOX

- Can weigh as much as 28 lb (12.7 kg)
- Lives for up to 12 years
- Needs up to 1 hour of exercise a day
- Happy in a small house or apartment

Did you know?

French Bulldogs are also known as "Frenchies" and sometimes even "Pigdogs," because they snort and love digging in the dirt, just like little piglets!

German Shepherd

Perfect puppy

The German Shepherd is one of the most popular dog breeds. Its huge ears and thick, shaggy coat make it instantly recognizable. German Shepherd puppies are especially cute with their oversized ears and feet. They will melt your heart!

Did you know?

An American soldier rescued a tiny German Shepherd puppy during World War I: the dog was named Rin Tin Tin and starred in 26 movies.

DOGGY NAPS

German Shepherds don't need very much sleep because they were bred to guard their flocks overnight.

🐾 Top dog

The breed began a long time ago as a herding dog in Germany. Since then, the German Shepherd has become so much more: it is used for police work, as a guard dog, a service dog, and a guide dog for the blind. German Shepherds are easy to train and are very caring.

FACT BOX

- 🐾 Can weigh as much as 95 lb (43.2 kg)
- 🐾 Lives for up to 14 years
- 🐾 Needs at least 2 hours of exercise a day
- 🐾 Loves a big house and large back yard

Golden Retriever

Perfect puppy

With their soft, golden hair, Golden Retrievers are very cute! The Golden Retriever keeps its happy, puppyish ways for a long time and loves to be with people. It likes to have a job, such as fetching the newspaper or a pair of slippers.

Did you know?

American Presidents Ford and Reagan both kept Golden Retrievers while they were in office.

🐾 Top dog

The Golden Retriever was bred as a working dog and was used by hunters to pick up and retrieve animals. Golden Retrievers are kind, friendly, and love to play!

FACT BOX

- 🐾 Weighs as much as 75 lb (34.1 kg)
- 🐾 Lives for up to 12 years
- 🐾 Needs more than 2 hours of exercise a day
- 🐾 Loves a large house and back yard

DOGGY NAPS

Some dogs like sleeping in a kennel, but Golden Retrievers love to sleep in the house with you!

Great Dane

🐾 Perfect puppy

Great Dane puppies might start out small, but they grow very quickly. The Great Dane is the biggest dog breed in the world! Though the Great Dane was bred to hunt wild boar, it is a sweet, gentle dog and it is very loving.

Did you know?

The biggest dog in the world is a Great Dane named Freddy who is 7 feet 6 inches (198 cm) tall if he stands on his hind legs!

🐾 Top dog

The first Great Dane was inspired by a Danish dog, but despite its name, the breed comes from Germany. It is sometimes called the "Apollo of dogs"—Apollo is the Greek god of the sun, the brightest star in the sky.

DOGGY NAPS

Great Danes are very big, but they will still try to curl up for a nap on your lap!

Hungarian Puli

Did you know?

In Hungary, there is a common color of the Puli which looks like the inside of a wholewheat bread roll.

🐾 Perfect puppy

This pup looks more like a floor mop than a dog! The loose curls of the Hungarian Puli puppy's coat join together as it gets older to form cords that look like dreadlocks. They form naturally, but can take as long as four years to grow. The cords make the dog look three times wider than it really is!

🐾 Top dog

The Puli is a very old breed, going back as far as 2,000 years. As Pulis were good at herding sheep, a good dog could cost a shepherd a whole year's wages. Hungarian shepherds were often very proud of their dogs.

DOGGY NAPS
The Puli never forgets that it is a herding dog and it will try to herd you, too, deciding when you should go to bed!

Irish Setter

 ## Perfect puppy

All setters are beautiful dogs and adorable puppies, but the glowing red coat of the Irish Setter is really special. Irish Setter puppies have a silky coat that lies close to their skin, but as they grow up their coat grows longer, and it ripples as they run around and play.

Did you know?
The first Irish Setters were called Red Spaniels or Modder Rhu, Gaelic for "red dog."

🐾 Top dog

Setters were bred to be gundogs that would track and retrieve birds. The early ones were red and white, but Irish Setters today are now plain red. Irish Setters are friendly, active, and sometimes mischievous!

FACT BOX

- 🐾 Can weigh as much as 70 lb (31.8 kg)
- 🐾 Lives for up to 15 years
- 🐾 Needs 2 hours of exercise a day
- 🐾 Loves a large house and back yard

DOGGY NAPS

Irish Setters adore people and would prefer to sleep in your bed than their own!

Labrador Retriever

DOGGY NAPS

Always eager to please, the Labrador will take itself off to bed when you do!

🐾 Perfect puppy

Many Labrador Retriever puppies are trained to become guide dogs for the blind because they are very gentle, smart, and kind. Labrador Retrievers love people, so they also make perfect family pets. The Labrador is caring and calm, with a short coat which needs little grooming.

Did you know?

The Labrador is the most popular dog in the United States and has been for the past 26 years.

🐾 Top dog

It takes its name from Newfoundland and Labrador, a part of northeast Canada. It was once called the St. John's dog after the capital city of Newfoundland, where it was used to help local fishermen with hauling nets, fetching ropes, and catching fish. Labrador Retrievers also make great rescue dogs.

Lhasa Apso

ZZZ Z

DOGGY NAPS
The Lhasa Apso snores a lot!

🐾 Perfect puppy

It may be small, but the Lhasa Apso thinks it's a big dog. Inside all that silky fluff, there is a tough little dog which, even as a puppy, can be quite fierce. Lhasa Apsos make excellent guard dogs as they have good observation skills and love to bark.

🐾 Top dog

The Lhasa Apso is named for the holy city of Lhasa, which is the capital of Tibet. It's a very old type of dog and was bred to be a watchdog in temples and monasteries. The little Lhasa Apso was thought to bring good luck.

FACT BOX

- 🐾 Can weigh up to 15 lb (6.8 kg)
- 🐾 Lives for up to 15 years
- 🐾 Needs up to 1 hour of exercise a day
- 🐾 Happy in an apartment

Did you know?
The first Lhasa Apsos came to the United States as gifts from the Dalai Lama.

Newfoundland

 ## Perfect puppy

This adorable breed looks like a teddy bear and is just as cuddly. The Newfoundland is very gentle, but also very strong. It loves children and will happily protect them from any sort of danger—it is a born babysitter!

DOGGY NAPS

The Newfoundland needs to be taught where it can sleep—it's not easy to pull a heavy dog off the couch!

 Top dog

Named for the northeast area of Canada, the Newfoundland worked with fishermen, helping to haul in their nets and swimming out to fetch items which fell from their boats. It also carried logs and worked as a rescue dog, pulling people out of the ocean.

Did you know?
The Newfoundland has a waterproof coat and webbed feet.

Old English Sheepdog

🐾 Perfect puppy

This delightfully shaggy dog is a born clown and stays puppylike until the age of three. It looks like a cuddly toy, but its hair grows quite long, and will need lots of brushing to keep it clean.

Did you know?

In the 1880s there were just five Old English Sheepdogs in the USA because they were very expensive.

FACT BOX

- 🐾 Can weigh as much as 80 lb (36.4 kg)
- 🐾 Lives for up to 12 years
- 🐾 Needs 2 hours of exercise a day
- 🐾 Loves a big back yard but can adapt to smaller spaces

🐾 Top dog

It is an old breed which was used to herd sheep and drive cattle to market. It is a big, strong dog, but is gentle and loving as well. Though it might not be the best guard dog, the Old English Sheepdog has a loud, deep bark to warn you of intruders.

53

Papillon

🐾 Perfect puppy

The fringed ears of this little dog give it its name. The word papillon is French for "butterfly"—the dog's upright ears look like a butterfly's outspread wings. It is elegant, dainty, and very sure of itself! Papillons are friendly and charming but can be very lively.

Did you know?

There is another version of this breed called the Phalene, whose ears look like the wings of a moth.

🐾 Top dog

The Papillon was once known as the Dwarf Spaniel and was very popular in the royal courts of Europe. Papillons are happy and friendly little dogs that are also very intelligent. They may be small, but they love long walks and are very energetic.

FACT BOX

- 🐾 Can weigh as much as 9 lb (4.1 kg)
- 🐾 Lives for up to 16 years
- 🐾 Needs 30 minutes of exercise a day
- 🐾 Happy in an apartment

DOGGY NAPS

For a little dog the Papillon has lots of energy and is more likely to want to play than have a snooze.

Pekingese

DOGGY NAPS

The Pekingese has very vivid dreams and will snort, snore, and sometimes bark in its sleep.

 ## Perfect puppy

From the moment it is born, the Pekingese—or Peke—knows it is special. This little dog has centuries of noble blood, and it has never forgotten. Even as a puppy, the Peke is bold and proud.

Did you know?

In China, owners would carry tiny Pekingese in the sleeves of their robes, so they became known as "sleeve dogs."

🐾 Top dog

The Pekingese history goes back a long time—to the Tang dynasty in China. The dog lived in the palaces of Peking (now Beijing) from where it took its name. The Pekingese has a lovely long, straight coat and a furry mane around its neck.

FACT BOX

- 🐾 Can weigh as much as 14 lb (6.4 kg)
- 🐾 Lives for up to 15 years
- 🐾 Needs 30 minutes of exercise a day
- 🐾 Happy in a small house or apartment

Pomeranian

DOGGY NAPS

Pomeranians can't handle extreme temperatures and they like their bed to be the perfect balance between hot and cold.

🐾 Perfect puppy

With its round eyes, foxlike face, and happy grin, the Pomeranian is a very cute puppy. But don't be fooled by its dainty looks, this is a tough and determined little dog. It knows very well how cute it is, and thinks it can get away with anything!

Z Z Z Z

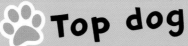 Top dog

The Pomeranian is one of the smallest breeds. Its name comes from Pomerania in northern Europe. It is a cute, little dog with pricked ears, an alert expression, and a thick coat.

FACT BOX
- Can weigh as much as 7 lb (3.2 kg)
- Lives for up to 16 years
- Needs 30 minutes of exercise a day
- Loves a small apartment

Did you know?
Two Pomeranians survived the sinking of the Titanic.

Poodle

DOGGY NAPS
Poodles love to sleep and will take several naps during the day!

🐾 Perfect puppy

A Poodle puppy is a fluffy little bundle of fun. Poodles are affectionate, loving dogs and they make great family pets. They are also very smart and easy to train. Circuses even used to teach them to perform tricks!

Did you know?
In Germany, the poodle is called *pudelhund*, which means "water dog."

- 🐾 Weighs as much as 70 lb (31.8 kg)
- 🐾 Lives for up to 15 years
- 🐾 Needs up to 1 hour of exercise a day
- 🐾 Loves a small house or apartment

🐾 Top dog

Poodles love to be pampered! You may have seen the Poodle with its adorable haircut—curly fur on its chest and neck, and pom-poms on its feet and tail. But this style does have a purpose—it goes back to when the hunters used Poodles to fetch birds. The birds were often in freezing water and the hair on the Poodle's chest and joints kept it warm.

Pug

zzzzz

DOGGY NAPS
The Pug likes to sleep a lot and will even take a nap sitting upright.

 ## Perfect puppy

Pug puppies are tiny, playful, and very cute with their curled little tails. The Pug's wrinkled face looks a bit worried until it turns into a delighted doggy grin! It comes from China, where its owners were important people who were devoted to their little dogs.

Did you know?
A group of Pugs is called a "grumble"!

🐾 Top dog

If you take your Pug wherever you go, both of you will get a warm welcome. Everybody loves a Pug! It is a neat little dog that is happy to be with people. Its name comes from the Latin word for "fist"—*pugnus*—because its short, squashy face looks like a human fist.

FACT BOX

- Only weighs about 18 lb (8.2 kg), but gains weight easily
- Lives for up to 15 years
- Needs very little exercise but likes to play
- Loves a small house or cozy apartment

Saint Bernard

DOGGY NAPS
Saint Bernards love to drool during their naps!

🐾 Perfect puppy

Saint Bernard puppies may start small, but they grow up to be one of the largest breeds. The Saint Bernard is very gentle and loves cuddles and attention. It will join in with your games and pull a cart, or even a sled during the winter.

🐾 Top dog

The breed comes from the mountains of Switzerland and is named after a monk who, more than 1,000 years ago, founded a hospital to care for travelers on their journey through the Swiss Alps. Saint Bernard dogs were used to help rescue people in the snow. They love company and can get lonely when they are left alone.

FACT BOX

- 🐾 Weighs as much as 180 lb (81.8 kg)
- 🐾 Lives for up to 10 years
- 🐾 Needs about 1 hour of exercise a day
- 🐾 Happy in a medium-sized house

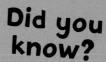

Did you know?

There is a Saint Bernard Pass in the Alps between Switzerland and Italy.

Samoyed

DOGGY NAPS
Samoyeds like to keep busy and be active, so they don't usually take naps as much as other dogs.

🐾 Perfect puppy

The Samoyed puppy looks like a cuddly toy with its white fluffy coat and happy smile. The breed was named after the Samoyede tribe and is pronounced "SAMmy-ed." Samoyeds love children and like to run around and play.

z z z z z

🐾 Top dog

The Samoyed is one of the world's oldest dog breeds. It comes from Siberia, where the Samoyede people used their lovely dogs to pull sleds, herd and guard reindeer, and protect them against predators. The dog has flat feet, like snowshoes, with thick hair to protect it from the cold.

FACT BOX

- Weighs as much as 60 lb (27.3 kg)
- Lives for up to 14 years
- Needs more than 2 hours of exercise a day
- Loves a large house and back yard

Did you know?

Samoyed fur can be spun and woven or knitted like wool into warm, soft clothing.

Schnauzer

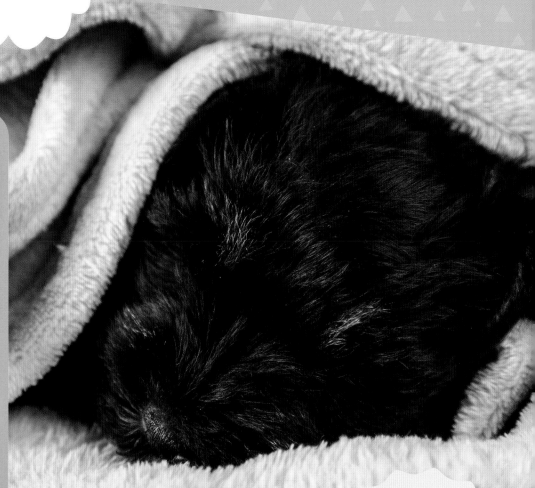

🐾 Perfect puppy

Schnauzer puppies are adorable with their black button noses and folded ears. They are also very smart. It's often said that the Schnauzer is a dog with a human brain.

Did you know?
The word "schnauzer" means "snout" in German.

🐾 Top dog

The Schnauzer comes from Germany, where it was used to guard livestock, herd cows and sheep, catch rats, and protect its owner. There are also miniature and giant versions of the breed which look similar with their fluffy eyebrows, bushy beards, and whiskers.

FACT BOX

- 🐾 Weighs as much as 50 lb (22.7 kg)
- 🐾 Lives for up to 16 years
- 🐾 Needs up to 1 hour of exercise a day
- 🐾 Loves a small house with a good-sized yard

DOGGY NAPS

Schnauzers can be very stubborn and need to learn when it's bedtime!

Shih Tzu

Z z z Z Z

 ## Perfect puppy

Shih Tzu puppies may be cute and fluffy, but in China where the breed was developed, its name means "little lion". Shih Tzus might look like lions with their long manes, but they aren't very fierce! They are friendly, gentle, and get along well with other dogs or animals.

Did you know?
Another name for the Shih Tzu is "chrysanthemum dog" because the hair on its face looks like the flower.

🐾 Top dog

The Shih Tzu is a very old breed and is thought to have been bred by monks in Tibet. It was kept by emperors in their palaces and treated like royalty. Shih Tzus are small dogs, but need regular grooming to keep their coats looking smooth and silky.

FACT BOX

- 🐾 Weighs as much as 16 lb (7.3 kg)
- 🐾 Lives for up to 16 years
- 🐾 Needs up to 1 hour of exercise a day
- 🐾 Happy in a small house or apartment

Siberian Husky

Did you know?
Siberian Huskies first came to North America in 1908 and pulled sleds during the Gold Rush.

🐾 Perfect puppy

With their sparkling, bright blue eyes and pretty markings on their faces, Siberian Husky puppies are very cute! From an early age, Siberian Huskies love to make new friends and don't like being left alone.

🐾 Top dog

The Husky has a beautiful, thick coat and is a very old breed. It comes from Siberia in Russia, where the native people, called Chukchi, used it to pull sleds through the snow. Huskies are very smart, strong, and can be very fast.

FACT BOX

- Weighs as much as 60 lb (27.3 kg)
- Lives for up to 15 years
- Needs 2 hours of exercise a day
- Loves a large house and back yard

DOGGY NAPS

To sleep, the Siberian Husky will tuck its nose under its bushy tail for warmth.

Tibetan Mastiff

🐾 Perfect puppy

With lots of thick fur and a swishing tail, the Tibetan Mastiff is a very cute puppy. But it grows, and grows, and grows! This old breed is one of the biggest dogs in the world and needs the right sort of home to be happy. It loves people, but it can be overprotective.

Did you know?

A Tibetan mastiff once sold for more than $1.2 million!

 ## Top dog

The Tibetan Mastiff comes from the Himalayan Mountains in Tibet, where its thick fur protected it from the cold. It guarded homes and livestock and was often left tied up outside the house to keep away intruders. It has a big, loud bark, too!

FACT BOX
- Weighs as much as 200 lb (91 kg)
- Lives for up to 14 years
- Needs up to 1 hour of exercise a day
- Loves a very big house and back yard

DOGGY NAPS
If the Tibetan Mastiff hears something during the night, it will wake up and bark!

Z Z Z z

Weimaraner

Did you know?

Weimaraner puppies are born with gray tiger stripes, but these fade within about three days.

🐾 Perfect puppy

Weimaraner puppies will grow up to be big dogs that need lots of exercise. The Weimaraner is known as the "silver ghost" because of the shimmery gray color of its coat. It is a pretty puppy, though its striking light gray, blue, or amber eyes can make it look a bit like a little alien!

🐾 Top dog

The Weimaraner was bred in Germany to hunt bear, wild boar, deer, and smaller animals like birds and rabbits. They are very smart, energetic, and love being part of an active family. Weimaraners also need a lot of attention.

DOGGY NAPS

Be prepared to take your Weimaraner to bed! They stick with their owner as much as they can.

Yorkshire Terrier

Did you know?

A Yorkshire Terrier named Sylvia held the record as the world's smallest dog. She was 2.5 inches (6.4 cm) tall, 3.5 inches (8.9 cm) long, and weighed only 4 ounces (113 g)!

🐾 Perfect puppy

These teeny, tiny puppies have lots of personality! With its long, silky hair, the Yorkshire Terrier knows it's a star and its small size means it can be carried around easily.

DOGGY NAPS

Yorkshire Terriers need lots of sleep—up to 17 hours a day!

🐾 Top dog

The Yorkshire Terrier was once known as the Broken-haired Scotch Terrier. The new name was adopted when the weavers of Scotland moved to the cotton mills of Yorkshire, England, and brought their tiny dogs with them. Yorkshire Terriers are always on the lookout for adventure and maybe even a bit of trouble...

FACT BOX
- 🐾 Weighs as much as 6 lb (2.7 kg)
- 🐾 Lives for up to 15 years
- 🐾 Needs up to 30 minutes of exercise a day
- 🐾 Loves a small house or apartment

Picture Credits

fc= front cover, bc=back cover, bg=background,
t=top, b=bottom, l=left, r=right, c=center